DIVINE

SHIFT

FROM RELIGION TO RELATIONSHIP

Visionary Author

JUANITA CORRY JACKSON

Published by Victorious You Press™

Printed in the United States of America

ISBN: 978-1-952756-03-0

For details email vyp.joantrandall@gmail.com
or visit us at www.victoriousyoupress.com

DEDICATION

In Loving Memory of

The Late Archbishop Matthew A. Barber

Thank you, sir, for the legacy you left us to follow and carry on. You started the charge of becoming an Author, for which you allowed me to walk by your side as Administrator. I can still remember the day you and I drove to the publishing company, picked out the book cover, signed the contract, and "God Is Not On Recess" was born.

From there, to walking beside you in ministry, I had no idea that you and God would be preparing me for my now season. Today! You would be proud that all your pastors and some new ministers are currently on the road to bestselling authors. Thank you for the wisdom you instilled me! I will never forget your teachings, the foundation which I stand today. This book is a dedication to your memory that still lives in us!

Juanita Corry Jackson,
I Believe God Ministries International

ACKNOWLEDGEMENTS

First, I want to begin with a thank you to God, who decided to use me to get the message out to the world of His Divine Shift!

I want to acknowledge these four amazing Authors who said yes to the commission of co-authors in this anthology, Angela Hope, Berthanna Oxendine, Valerie Rogers, and Deloris Washington. Ladies, you are all a gift from God. Thank you for taking a leap of faith in telling your stories, sharing your pain, and allowing us to rejoice with you in the Shift, the victory! To the ministry that God has given me the charge of being Overseer, I Believe God Ministries International, you guys are my tribe! I love you to life! Thank you to CT Collab for the beautiful photography sessions with the authors and making it such a fun experience. To my God-ordained Publishing Company, Victorious You Press, and all the staff from the Editor's to the Graphic Designers, the assistants in the background for making it happen, and CEO Joan T. Randall. Joan, thank you for hearing God's voice in your predesigned purpose of helping writers become bestselling authors.

To my children Demond Corry, Shareka Corry, and Kendra Jackson. My one and only granddaughter, Taniyah Corry. You guys are my rock, and you are the reason outside of God's directive that I do what I do. I want you always to know that you can do anything that you set your heart and mind to, as long as you keep God first in your lives. Everything that I am working to build is a legacy that will far outlive me, for you, your children, and children's children. You will forever be my ride to life crew!!

For every reader that will pick up this book, read and share with others, thank you! Thank you for every page you turn and decide to continue the journey with us. In the back of the book, we have added a link to how you can join our Facebook community, and in advance, I want to say thank you for becoming part of our Divine Shift Family!

FOREWORD

Joan T Randall

When I think about Juanita Corry Jackson, the phrase that comes to mind is a *"woman of substance."* It is hard to articulate what that means, but I will try to get as close as I can with my definition. A woman of substance is a woman of power, positive influence, and meaning. To break it down even further, her character qualities are peacefulness, love, patience, and steadfastness, to name a few. She possesses virtues that make others around her notice her character and integrity.

I met Overseer Jackson at an entrepreneurial event that I hosted, and we had an opportunity to meet up one on one at a later date. Our conversation was varied. We talked about our commonalties as entrepreneurs, our love for God, and the adversities we had faced in our lives. As we conversed, I was in awe of her grace, humility, and knowledge of God's word. Besides being passionate about teaching God's words, she also loves people and wants them to thrive spiritually, mentally, and financially. She has a passion for the underdog and the less fortunate; for those who have experienced a hard knock life. I truly admire that about her... it reminds me of Jesus.

We developed a great friendship as I soon realized that she was just the person I needed in my life as a spiritual Coach and Mentor.

I remembered vividly my conversation with Overseer Juanita Corry Jackson about Religion vs. Relationship and the effects it can sometimes have on people in the church. Her outlook and stance on the topic were so refreshing. It gave me a glimpse into the fabric of who she is and the anointing she has on her life as a Pastor and an agent for God. During this conversation, she talked about the laws and traditions that play a huge role in some churches. The fact that those traditions were sometimes based on what the generation before did or say. Rules were followed without spiritual guidance, and they were set in stone because the one before that, said it was so.

How many times have we heard scriptures quoted in the wrong context, but because it was taught, then it was followed. The need to study for oneself to understand it better was trumped by *"that's how it's always done."* Some faith-based institutions have allowed religion to take center stage over relationship, love, and care. Religion can come across as judgmental, especially if someone is outside of what the tradition mandates. God wants us to seek him with our hearts and not with rules.

In this book, Visionary Author Overseer Jackson and her co-authors open up about their realization of religion and the lack of relationship. They all grew up in the church, and they recognized that they were following those same traditions passed down to them.

It is not easy to break away from tradition, but they did and, as a result, found the peace of Jesus and the knowledge of what being like Him means. They transformed their need to be religious into operating in a spirit of love and care for everyone they come in contact with. They ditched the judgments based on looks, clothes, expectations, rules, and activated Christ's love and the spirit of a beautiful relationship built on Faith, Hope, Care, and Love. I applaud them for being transparent in sharing.

Don't miss the critical points in these stories. And as you go through each of them, pause, answer the guided questions and reflect on your journey. Relationships are about connections. Are you still stuck in a tradition of religion with all the rules? Or can you, will you, move forward with meaningful relational connections based on faith and love.. Trust me, the latter will make others want to connect with you.

Bravo to Janita Corry Jackson and the authors of this book, which is so appropriate for such a time as this.

CONTENTS

INTRODUCTION

There was a clarion call that arrived early one morning when I was not quite sure if it was day or night. A mandate from Heaven had arrived. I kept hearing, *It is a Divine Shift.* This call is not for me I am sure, maybe, just maybe this call arrived at the wrong address. I remember turning over, and back to sleep I went. A small voice kept saying, it must be five, it must be five. Now I am sure I am not going to get any more sleep on this morning. So, I ask, "What does it mean God? What are you saying? Are we on a sermon preparation journey?" Yes, He would answer, but not in the way you think. This in fact, I would learn is a life lesson and a life message. It would become a journey, a journal, of past pain, present plans, and a future to prosper in every area of my life.

Let's digress a little. Divine Shift was all about a Shift within our spiritual, emotional, and financial wellness. It would become a book of life lessons that five different authors would come together and write. God had challenged us to tell our stories of how we had been and are being delivered from Religion to Relationship. Religion is a set of manmade rules, intertwined with our faith. In religion however, we end up with more rules than faith. After all, the two are always at odds with each other, right? The rule says this is the way it is. It has always been done this way, and it must always be done the exact same way. Faith is just the opposite. Faith says, you don't need to see it, it does not even need to exist yet, just believe. Faith is the substance of things hoped for; which literally means faith has the power to turn something that does not exist yet, into substance, something that is in fact real.

As God began to impart the instructions for this book, the first thing He said was, "Five authors." Five represents the number for Grace, and His Grace is always sufficient. Whatever lacks in me, or in the authors, His Grace is sufficient. As you begin to turn the pages of each one of our stories, and work alongside us in the lessons within the pages, please know that for you too, His grace is sufficient. He is waiting for us all within the pages of this book. It will be an adventure, your ticket for the journey has already been prepaid by God Himself. The travel time is self-paced. While the authors have structured the trip as thirty-one days, there are no rules necessary. Take as little time or as long as you want. Complete and start again if you so desire. For some of us the journey may be a day long, others a week, and yet for others who are life learners, the journey never ends.

You may say, "Well, this book, this trip is not for me. I am in church. I have a relationship. I love the Lord" Perhaps you might be right, but watch the caution sign just ahead of you. In the bible, the Pharisees and Sadducees had the same thoughts with all their rules,

2

and even wore their devout church gear, and preached about the coming Messiah. Yet, when Jesus came, they did not recognize Him and was instrumental in putting Jesus on the cross.

Let me just set the record straight for all the authors; we all grew up in church, all from different backgrounds, our storms, the rules, of which we lived by were all different, yet the same. As we began to put words to paper, all the authors who lived in different states and or areas of town, seemed as if our paths had crossed, as if we had lived in the same house, or for sure, on the same street. That is how Grace works. God keeps you, favors you, and preserves you for His Glory.

At the writing of this introduction, God said this SHIFT is for every person that will hear His voice. It does not matter if you live in a crack house or the white house, or any place in between. God loves you and wants you whole. I would dare to say, that no matter where we are in life, there are some old wounds lying beneath the surface that are just lying dormant, perhaps. The problem with hidden wounds is on the surface we can ignore that they are there, until that same spot is pricked, and then, the wound will erupt. Eruption is sometimes what we have labeled as "church hurt," meaning something might have been distasteful, downright wrong, or just plain ignorance that happened in a church building. Underneath that, however, is one person typically, who in and of themselves are flawed as we all are, and most often we relate those incidents back to the church at large, and sometimes even God Himself.

Church hurt, or religious rules, are not the only kind of rules that cause us to ignore the hidden wounds. There is also, "What happens *in this house, stays in this house"* mentality *or "This is the way it has always been, and this is the way it will always be."* Then, there is the rule of shame, *"I do not want anyone to know that it happened to me".* I could list those out forever. Rather than list them here, join us throughout the lessons and list your own. This book, this journal, this road trip, whatever label you put on it, be brave, be courageous enough to go with us. I call it, as mandated by God, a "Divine Shift."

Time to travel! Grab your bag as we go through this shift together. If you are holding this book, God's Grace has stamped your prepaid ticket, and you are ready to board. He preplanned this even before the beginning of time, just as He brought all the authors and me together, in this way, He also planned that our paths would cross, if only in the pages of this book; but who knows, it's not over yet. Bring your tissues, maybe grab a pillow, or a prayer shawl, if you have one. You will also, want to pack your favorite pen, highlighter, and a writing pad to take some notes of your own.

In Divine Shift, according to Webster Dictionary, a **shift** is a change in something or an adjustment in the way something is done. But, a **divine shift** is a supernatural move from one place to another, a slight change in position or direction; the supernatural act of putting one thing in the place of another or changing the place of a person or thing. Inside this book, you will see the change that happens for the Authors, bruises healed, pain, hurt, disappoint, and just plain old contentment, shifted. Lean into the small window of our stories and watch the transformation. I have no doubt that you will catch a glimpse of your story too.

A Prayer for The Readers

Dear God, thank you for just being God! In your Word, you tell us that we can ask whatever we will, and it shall be given unto us.

My prayer today is for every person that will hold this book in their hand, that you will give them page by page more wisdom and insight into their journey. Father, if their stories get hard to face, you would encourage them to do it anyway. All things through your strength are possible. Please give them the vision to see, the strength to write, the encouragement to surrender, the grace to forgive, and the power to shift! I call for your grace and mercy to meet us in every sentence, every paragraph, and page. Let the words that you have caused these authors to write, not be finished here, but each reader will begin to compose their own stories within the pages of the journal and hear your voice speak throughout the stories. Thank you, God! I am giving you praise right now in faith that you will answer yes and amen to this prayer. So, I count it done in the Mighty Name of Jesus, my Lord, and Savior! Amen!

FORGIVENESS A PATHWAY TO RELATIONSHIP

Deloris J Washington

Let us think back to something we can all relate to, remember as a child, when a sibling or friend did something to hurt or make you angry? You were asked by a parent to forgive them. The offender had to say, "I'm sorry." It was said with a pouty demeanor, looking down and not at the offended, and you had to respond by saying, "I forgive you." But thinking, "I will never forget."

Religion began for me as a child. I was taught about God's love, forgiveness, and His care for me in the throes of Jim Crow Law. My Mom had just transitioned from Religion to Divine Relationship shortly before I was born. So, unforgiveness and hatred was not part of my upbringing in word or deed. The Golden Rule was always stressed; you must treat others the way you want to be treated.

Several unpleasant things happened in my family during my pre-teen years that caused shame, anger, and hurt. I had been an eyewitness to a traumatic incident. The revelation of this action in a small town, would have caused untold hurt to our family. My Mom and Dad chose to be forgiving, moving forward, restoring, and bringing the family back together. As a child, I didn't understand forgiveness on that level. My parents encouraged me to trust God for healing for all family members. We moved forward to embrace those who had caused hurt. I began to understand the power and restoration forgiveness can bring. No sin is so great that one cannot be forgiven and move on to restoration, wholeness, and new life.

Shortly after marriage, my husband and I became involved in a wonderful church, slightly different from my parents'. Acknowledging one's need for forgiveness was the first step toward a relationship with God. Our journey in this church was intense. We were happy and very involved in Bible studies, a clean lifestyle, a strict dress code, and activities. Frequent church attendance was required. We thought we had a relationship with God. I always felt something was missing. I began to feel more and more empty. I sought to fill the emptiness by looking deeper into the pathway that God had designed for us to have a relationship with Him; not just some approach of do's and don'ts.

When I moved to a Divine Relationship, it was through a better understanding of what God had done for me and all humanity. The Gospels teach us about the ministry of Jesus on earth and His instructions to humanity. The Book of Acts gives us further pathways to God. The Second Chapter presents Old Testament history, and its fulfillment, the approach to God by grace and not ritual. The ultimate sacrifice by Jesus Christ has now been paid.

The instructions began with "repent" (ask forgiveness) and wash away your sin; He will come in and empower you to live a life of a divine relationship. The Spirit of God comes to dwell in you. Following this pathway from the heart, I moved from Religion to Divine Relationship. A divine relationship is an ongoing perfecting relationship with God because you now understand the Love of God for you. You begin to walk in divine power and love for Him, and not mere "do's and don'ts."

I found myself in a conflict with a family member. This family member was in Religion, and I decided they were not happy with me, and I was not the only person in which they were unhappy. They would belittle and undermine my testimony. We had a great relationship despite that. We did many things together, and I was always there for them. I was not walking in unforgiveness, or so I thought. It was anger. The continual stabs in the heart in front of others, hurt and fueled my anger again, and again. I made up excuses for why this kept happening and chose to move forward with life and continue our relationship as usual. However, I wanted to get over this anger once and for all, this went on for many years. I finally decided to confront them with how I felt. Perhaps they were unaware of the hurt I was feeling. So, with a humble attitude I gave them the benefit of the doubt that maybe, they were unaware of my feelings. We had a successful talk, prayer, and purpose to be mindful of words, deeds, and the effect they may have. But, from time to time, it continued, and I felt that anger rise in me. I prayed, fasted, and tried to make excuses for them. The anger prevailed after each stab in the heart.

Finally, victory came at a Ladies Conference. The final session was about moving forward in times of being offended by others, be it the workplace, family members, friends, or those closest to you. I was so desperate to get rid of this anger. In this session, they asked us to take a string from the many strings that were placed on the altar ahead of time. We were to exchange our string with someone we did not know. The string represented the one thing we wanted to be delivered from. We were not to tell our prayer partner what it represented. We exchanged our strings at the end of the lesson.

My prayer partner prayed for me and said words that related to my problem; things she could not have known. After a time of prayer for each other, we took our strings and laid them on the altar. I felt a powerful, refreshing, release; the physical act of giving it to God. The mental act of giving it to God, I had not done. The stabs continued from time to time, but I never felt the anger again, no matter what was said.

So, my devotion for today is forgiven, forgive, and forgiveness. As we stop to investigate true forgiveness, we see the forethought of God. GOD PLANNED Forgiveness before He formed the earth. Revelation 13:8 speaks of the lamb slain before the earth was formed. What an awesome realization. God had already prepared to forgive humankind. Forgiveness and the need to be forgiven is a heart-wrenching emotion, not just thinking it in your head or repeating after someone. And now you are saved. Remember back to that childhood example, the painful saying, "I'm sorry." No one can say it for you. True repentance is the first step. It is Acknowledging you have done wrong and are in need of the forgiveness that only God gives.

When Adam and Eve sinned, God came to them; they did not run to Him. They hid and blamed each other for the sin when confronted. God knew, and He forgave them. He prepared coverings for them by slaying an animal. In Genesis 3:21, the face to face fellowship ended for man in the garden with a promise of one who would come. Jesus, the Man, would be the sacrifice for humanity. "In the fulfillment of time, John the Baptist saw Jesus coming to be baptized, and he proclaimed, 'Behold the Lamb of God which taketh away the sin of the world'" John 1:29. This verse reminds us of the sacrifice of Jesus that affords restoration of man and offers a personal relationship with Him, if a man chooses. It is man's choice to make.

What is your view of sin? Many say I am a good person and give many reasons why they think they are good and acceptable in God's sight. There are no degrees in sin. Romans 3:23 says, "All have sinned and come short of the Glory of God." We must line up to God's pathway to forgiveness. To forgive and forget or move on is difficult to do with the overpowering mindset of "Why me?" or "They don't deserve to be forgiven." In our present-day, we see the trend to judge, punish, and never allow for second chances.

The vilest act of sin is seen the same as someone who lives a "good life." They are both in need of God's forgiveness and must acknowledge it by words of repentance from the heart. We must see the lack of God's provision for a restored relationship. It is the forgiveness of God that allows the pathway to eternal life. It does not matter how vile you have been. We are all equal in the sight of God as sinners. Forgiveness is an action we must take. According to Matthew 6:12, "We will be forgiven, because we forgive." Read the instructions for the good life in Matthew 6:9-15. We seek forgiveness, but many times we are quick to withhold forgiveness from others. Forgiveness sets us free. In Matthew 6:14, we receive benefits when we forgive.

When we enter Divine Relationship, we acknowledge we have sinned and need forgiveness as we desire to be in a relationship with God—walking in agreement with God—understanding His plan for our life. This request comes from the heart, not just random words, because someone told you to say them. Matthew 11:28-30 tells us how to find rest for our soul. We have the privilege to walk in relationship with Him after true repentance. We become enlightened to His word and realize that offenses will come, as offenses are meant to make us strong. We must have some testing to become useful in the kingdom of God to the saving of others. Sometimes even the people who have offended us, may be the ones we can share our great story of salvation to, thereby saving their soul.

Perhaps you are someone who may have done terrible things or caused offenses. We all have an open pathway to God to be forgiven. "If we confess our sins, He is faithful and just to forgive us our sins, and to cleanse us from all unrighteousness" (1 John 1:9). Think about those two powerful words, faithful and just. Isaiah 43:25 tells us that He will take away our sins and will not remember them anymore. How great is that? We will indeed remember offenses, but the knowledge of God's love for us and our relationship with Him takes away the sting of offenses, and we can reach out to the offender in genuine love. The good news is we can walk in restoration and Devine Relationship

What happens if I don't forgive? Emotions like anger, envy, hatred, and bitterness are the pathway downward to unforgiveness. In a divine relationship, the pathway becomes forgiven, forgive, and forgiveness. God forgives you, and you are to forgive others because you now walk in forgiveness. You may not ever forget, but the sting of hurt will be covered in the light of God's forgiving you, and the reality of the Divine Relationship you now walk in. The scripture in Ephesians 4:32 tells us what manner of people we now are because we have been forgiven.

Do you think you can become the person that God says you can? Romans 12:9-20 and James 3:14-18 tells us to walk in Divine Relationship. Also, l John chapter 3 tells us what manner of people we should be since we have now been forgiven and walk-in Divine Relationship. We are now called the sons of God. We walk in hope and keep ourselves pure and clean in our daily walk with Him.

We know that God has designed all things for our restoration to walk with Him in Divine Relationship. We can walk in freedom, peace, and love. The bible also tells us to be kind, tenderhearted, and forgiving each other. Why? Because God has forgiven you. We can trust God's pathway to a forgiving life. He designed all things for our restoration, to walk with Him, from the very beginning, and enjoy Divine Relationship. Calvary allows us to walk with Him in freedom, peace, and love into eternity. God never asked us to do anything beyond our capability. Our present life and eternity hinges on forgiven, forgive, forgiveness. It's a free choice, but necessary for all mankind. Jesus provided the pathway to this freedom of the heart and redemption of the soul, to walk In Divine Relationship.

Date: _____

Lesson One: Discovery
Discovery and Reflection Journal
FORGIVENESS TO PATHWAY TO RELATIONSHIP

In this chapter, let us review what resonated about the Author's story with you and why.

In the beginning of the journey the Author grew up in a Christian home, and still had to go through steps of forgiveness. What did you learn about yourself from the story?

Date: _____

Lesson Two: Reflection
Discovery and Reflection Journal
FORGIVENESS TO PATHWAY TO RELATIONSHIP

Has there been a time you found forgiveness hard? How did you handle it?

For the Author, she found the true release came through a conference and releasing a string of rope on the alter. How did you find your release, or how will you seek to have freedom in releasing?

Date: _____

Lesson Three: The Journey
Discovery and Reflection Journal
FORGIVENESS TO PATHWAY TO RELATIONSHIP

If you found the above exercise and this chapter helpful, what has it taught you about yourself and about God and Forgiveness?

Date: _____

Lesson Four: The Shift
Discovery and Reflection Journal
FORGIVENESS TO PATHWAY TO RELATIONSHIP

After reading this chapter, what lesson can you use to shift your life or the life of others towards forgiveness.

Date: _____

Lesson Five: The Relationship
Discovery and Reflection Journal
FORGIVENESS TO PATHWAY TO RELATIONSHIP

You made it another step on a "Divine Shift." How can Forgiveness help you to develop or increase your relationships through forgiveness?

CHOOSE TO LOVE

Bishop Valerie J. Rogers

As a young child, I can still, to this day, remember living with my grandparents in North Carolina. My grandfather worked in Tennessee in the tobacco market, only getting to come home every three months. It was my grandmother who was left to care for me most of the time.

My grandparents were both great providers, loving, and supportive. My grandfather would come home as often as possible, with a great big smile and open arms. Now, my grandmother on the other hand, was the disciplinarian, but was very loving. She was a devout Christian woman who loved the Lord with her whole heart. She attended school up to the third grade leaving her unable to read or write. While there may have been limitations in her life in the natural, she was not limited spiritually.

From a small child, I remember her taking me to church every Sunday morning and to most evening services. As I grew older, I remember when my mother would come to see me for one week during the summer and then at Christmas. Christmas was a big time for me; I would get lots of toys and other lovely things. I could hardly wait for each time she would come to see me, but it was over just as fast as it happened, and then, she was gone again. The tears would start to roll down my face because I wanted to go back with her. I began to feel that she did not love or even want me.

I was so angry with her because I could not understand why; I would ask myself the question over and over in my mind, why didn't she want me? All the other kids I knew lived with their mommies; why couldn't I live with mine? I remember the times when I would fall and hurt myself; I just wanted my mother there to kiss it and make it better, but that would not happen until the next Christmas when she would come to see me.

I started to resent her coming and disliked the other kids whose mothers were there for them. My grandmother was so good to me; she would cook a hot breakfast for me each morning before I would leave for school. She made sure all of my needs were taken care of; I never wanted for anything, other than my mother. One day, my grandmother explained that my mother couldn't take care of me living in New York.

Sarah, my grandmother, was the best thing that ever happened for and to me. She had a love of Jesus, and she had that unwavering faith in Jesus. She went from talking JESUS to living JESUS. It went from just having Religion to a genuine relationship with Him. The definition of "**Religion**" in the most comprehensive sense includes a belief in the being and perfections of God, in the revelation of his will to man, and in man's obligation to obey his commands or in a state of reward and or punishment.

Jesus was my grandmother's all in all, and she would talk to me about how much she loved and trusted Him for everything. With everything she poured into me about the love of Jesus, my grandmother told me how I must obey God, keep his commandments, and trust Him, no matter my age. There was no way to tell her about all the anger I felt against my mom. How could I ever tell her that I wanted to leave her and go live with my mother? I was angry with my mother, but I still wanted to be with her.

I thank God for the many years that I lived with my grandmother, how she instilled in me the love of God—teaching me to love everybody regardless of the color of their skin or where they lived. In all that my grandmother taught me, none hit home like the scripture, "Honor thy father and thy mother that thy days may be long upon the land which the Lord thy God giveth thee," (Exodus 20:12). Being as young as I was, I was having a battle within. The bible says in Jeremiah 29:11, "For I know the thoughts that I think toward you, saith the Lord, thoughts of peace, and not of evil, to give you an expected end." Little did I know how this passage of scripture would play out in my life.

While I was excited about my freedom, it would be two years before I would ever reach that goal from the lady I only knew at Christmas. One day I got upset with my grandmother and I told her that I wanted to go home and live with my mother.

She said, "Okay, I will pack your stuff."

I was shocked by what she said, and then I wanted to stay, but I wanted to go and be with my mother. I knew it hurt my grandmother, but I was now free to leave. I wanted the best of both worlds, only finding myself crying many days until I finally left.

When I left that small town in North Carolina and arrived in New York City, it was scary to a little country girl. My time finally had come; I was now living with my mother. Everything was different where she lived, including the school I was attending, and even the food tasted different. New York was a large city, and the people weren't too friendly, it seemed. Now, I had been living with my mother for three years, and there were many nights I wanted to go back to my grandmother's, only to hear her say to me, "I told you so." My mother didn't go to church the first three years I lived with her, and I wasn't used to that. My grandmother raised me to go to church every Sunday. I could hear my grandmother when she would be praying for me, asking the Lord to lead and guide me and keep me from all danger. God used this woman to push me toward my future in Him and live a life according to His will.

One day while sitting outside with a friend, she invited me to go to church with her and her family. My friend was being raised by her father and grandmother; they were extremely strict. I started going with them to church, and it was different from what I was familiar with; I was used to the shouting or the Holy dance because my grandmother shouted every Sunday. However, at my friend's church, they had the gift of speaking in tongues, and I did not understand what they were saying. It seemed as if this was the start of a new life, one I never knew before. It went from praying with my mouth to praying in the spirit.

At the age of fifteen, I accepted Christ as Lord and Savior, and my whole life began to change. My thinking had changed, and I no longer wondered about Him, but I came to know Him as Lord. I became one in Christ, now having a genuine connection in Him. As I grew more in Christ, my relationship with Him became more real to me. I could not wait to go back to church to hear the word over again; it was a joy to my soul. I wanted what everyone else had at that church. I later became a member of the church, and I started seeking the Holy Spirit. The bible teaches us to have confidence in him. Philippians 1:6 says, "Being confident of this very thing, that he which hath began a good work in you will perform it until the day of Jesus Christ" (KJSB). After I received the Holy Spirit, and my journey had begun, I had to become more confident, knowing that He would work in my life and that He would get the glory. Now more than ever, I realized Christian life is far more than just my convictions; it includes my conduct and character. It's no longer what I think or feel, but it's according to His word. The one thing I was beginning to understand more was that Christianity is not a religion, but a relationship and a lifestyle. The bible says in Galatians 2:20, "Nevertheless, I live; yet not I, but Christ that liveth in me."

This new relationship that I had found in Him, has led me to a higher height and a more profound desire to serve Him. The more I received from His word, the more I wanted of Him. The bible tells us in St. Mark 11:24, "Therefore I say unto you, what things soever ye desire when ye pray, believe that ye receive them, and ye shall have them." This passage of scripture empowered me to have faith to believe I could ask, and I would receive it. That was powerful to me in that He would not withhold any good thing from me.

Therefore, when you ask, according to His will, you shall receive it. For His will to be done, we must have faith in God that those things which he saith shall come to pass, and we shall have whatsoever he saith.

I never returned to my grandmother's, but her words and teaching continued to flood my mind daily. When I would speak to her on the phone, she would ask me if I was going to church every Sunday, and what church I was attending. She would remind me of the things she had taught me, and that Jesus loves me. I missed her hugs and her telling me how much she loved me. That old saying, "Absence makes the heart fonder," I now understand it a little better; that leaving my grandmother developed our relationship. The bible reminds us in Philippians 4:13, "I can do all things through Christ, which strengtheneth me." No matter what the confrontation in my life, it is because of my relationship with Him that I can trust Him to deliver me out of them all. Even though my relationship with my mother never developed to the level in which I felt that she loved me, deep down within, I knew she loved me, but she showed no affection. I continued to try and understand why she didn't have time or wouldn't take the time to show me the love I needed and wanted.

We all have a choice, and God does not override our will. When I answered the call from God and asked Him to come into my heart, that was the day I committed myself to Him. My mother had the same upbringing as me. She also learned God's love. So, I couldn't understand why she was unable to show love and affection. The choice to return to God was up to her.

As I began to learn and understand that God is a spirit, and they that worship Him must worship Him in Spirit and Truth, I continued to pray for my mother, asking God to bring her back to Him and save her. Above all else, I knew that God is a prayer-answering God, that whatsoever I ask in faith, believing He will hear me. Romans 8:28 states, "And we know that in all things God works for the good of those who love Him, who have been called according to His purpose." The bible encourages me when I endure heartaches and sufferings in this world. He will help me.

After I had gotten saved, I went to church as often as my mother would allow me to go. Things started to get worse between my mother and me. Oftentimes, she would not let me go to church because she did not understand my walk with the Lord. She did not understand the baptism in the Holy Spirit and why I wanted to go to church. I remembered hearing my mother and stepfather arguing over me going to church, and he would often take up for me and would tell her to leave me alone.

I felt as if I had gone from one painful ordeal to another. The Word said that in all things, God would work for the good of those who love him. I love the Lord with my whole heart, soul, and body. I went from wanting to feel the affection of my mother to wanting the freedom to worship Him in Spirit and Truth. The Lord kept me.

Sometimes we may have felt as if He was not listening or hearing our cries, but God does. He promised never to leave us nor forsake us nor His seed begging bread. Time soon passed and I graduated high school and got married. It was not until I moved to Tennessee where my grandmother had moved, that we were reunited. Several years later, my mother and stepfather moved to Tennessee also. I had invited my mother to come to the church I was attending, and the Lord allowed her to experience his Holy Spirit. What a change that took place in her life on that day, she was never the same. It was with many tears shed when she asked me to forgive her. It was with great joy that I did.

Date: _____

Lesson One: Discovery
Discovery and Reflection Journal
Choose to Love

In this chapter, let's review the process of the choice of love. When you look in the small window of Bishop Rogers's journey, did you find her in love or angry?

What was the root of her anger or love in the story?

Date: _____

Lesson Two: Reflection

Discovery and Reflection Journal
Choose to Love

Now reflect on your own story and discover where you are within your journey. Reflect on yourself as far back as your childhood, see if things are hurting you in your present. Perhaps for you, it might not be abandonment, but list them out here.

For Bishop Rogers, her Mother had left her with her grandparents to raise. From the Mother's perspective, perhaps it was the best she could do for her daughter at the time, but from a little girl's perspective, it was devastating. Forgiveness is often the first step to loving yourself and others on a higher conscience level. List any persons, including yourself, that you can be brave enough to forgive, and remember that forgiveness does not erase what happened but gives you the freedom to live past it.

Date: _____

Lesson Three: The Journey

Discovery and Reflection Journal
Choose to Love

If you found there are people you need to forgive, including yourself, or if you are still holding on to anger, begin the journey by writing a letter to the person or addressing the situation and explain the pain you believe they caused you, or you think you caused.

Date: _____

Lesson Four: The Shift

Discovery and Reflection Journal
Choose to Love

You took a bold step in all the lessons above, if you were brave enough to do the work. It is time now to begin the shift. In lesson three, most likely, it brought up some pain, maybe opened some old wounds. However, this is not the place to stay, let's take out the pen and paper again, and this time write, "I forgive you." It is not as hard as you think; it's really a surrender. Forgiveness is necessary to begin the healing process and a place to build upon for you. So now that we have acknowledged it, let us forgive it.

Date: _____

Lesson Five: The Relationship

Discovery and Reflection Journal
Choose to Love

You made it, now choose to Love. What did you learn about how the Author's story shifted? What did you learn about your own story, and was there a recognizable shift? Today, let us write out our prayer to God of how our relationship with Him, ourselves, and the people around us that we are called to love can be better, intentional.

THE TINY SCAR THAT HEALED

Minister Angela A. Hope

My little, bony knees would hurt so bad during prayer. Sometimes one of the sweet little mothers would give me an old dusty pillow for me to kneel on, which would help ease the pain. But I loved to pray. My parents were always conducting the openings of the various services with singing praise and testimonies of how good God is. I loved seeing the saints rejoice when someone would share about the goodness of Jesus. It wasn't until I got older that I realized just how much of a significant role my parents played in the ministry. What was great about this was my home was an extension of what I felt in the church. There was plenty of joy, peace, and love in my house. My parents always demonstrated the love of God at home, just as they did at church.

So, let's talk about religion. I must admit growing up I didn't know the difference. I didn't even know religion existed. Going to church was just a part of life for me, and probably for most of us. I don't recall that it ever bothered me to go to church. Besides, I loved how singing, clapping my hands, and preaching made me feel. The tall, gray-haired pastor was always screaming, and hollering, and wore a long black robe. It was so exciting, even if I didn't understand everything he was preaching. While there was good teaching in Sunday school and a great Sunday morning sermon, I still remembered hearing about going to that bad place called hell if you weren't a good person or didn't live right. Do you remember hearing those sermons? Did you feel scared? I sometimes did. I guess it was a mixture of excitement and feeling scared all at the same time.

You know Matthew 19:14 states, "Jesus said, Let the little children come to me, and do not hinder them, for the kingdom of heaven belongs to such as these." As a young girl, it was the innocence of being a child that allowed the Holy Spirit to flow through me. I was baptized in the name of Jesus as a teenager, and that water sure felt so good and refreshing. I came up out of the water praising God! But as I became a young adult, the love and genuine religious experience grew dim. I allowed sin to creep in. I began to desire and wanted to experience what the church folks said was the "world" and the things they taught were sin.

I could not participate in school activities, wear pants, or listen to good clean secular music. All these things were considered immoral, and you would go to hell if you did anything wrong. Can you imagine? I must say that not participating in school activities sort of took me over the edge. As a teenager, this started to not sit well with me. Something didn't feel right. That is when things changed for me.

Fast forward, I have always known that the Lord and I had a special relationship. Isn't that just like God to love us and meet us right where we are, just like He did with the Samaritan woman at the well in John 4:4-26. This story depicts that Jesus was a relational man. But back to the story, it was a long ten years or more living without Jesus being the head of my life, but I knew He was always with me. In troubled times, I remember those scriptures from my childhood and the word of God that would overshadow me and be the sweetest comfort to my soul. Even when hanging out with my girls partying, I was the one who would always say a prayer first. It became the norm, and someone would say, "Ok, Angela, go ahead, pray before we hit the streets."

My parents were, now, attending a new church that was predominately white with a white pastor, but for me it was returning to an old-fashioned altar. The church was near Andrews Airforce Base in Camp Springs, Maryland. Families of all nationalities were always coming and going. Everyone wore long dresses with their hair pinned up like pilgrims and plain faces without a drop of makeup in sight. It seemed to be okay at first. This church was very different from the church where I originally grew up. I was so happy to feel the Holy Ghost's presence after many years of exploring sin in the worst way; I was okay with just having a sense of peace. I met some lovely people, some who are my friends today. They loved my parents and loved our family. Let me make this very clear. I felt like this was a safe place, because I thought if these people could strip down to nothing, which I thought was an act of purity, then I was in the right place. But as time would have it, they began to expose themselves. Not all of them were the good, clean Christians I thought they were. I could see the religious mindset in them growing bigger and bigger as the church was growing.

You see, while I was growing into an authentic relationship with Christ, not because I was scared to go to hell or because of what my parents had taught me, I had some horrific experiences when I left the church for a while. I knew it was only God's grace, love, and mercy that wrapped me in His arms and pulled me out of a terrible situation. It was clear that something was changing. I was considered a woman of faith or a religious person to the world, but not saved enough in the church. Not to mention, I felt like I was not true to who God fearfully and wonderfully made me to be. I felt in bondage and didn't feel free overtime trying to keep up with the church's rules, stipulations, and politics. And during all of that, I was a choir member, a member of the prayer team, team C that is. There was an A, B, and C altar call prayer team.   The C prayer team was very seldom called to pray with the souls at the altar, but I continued to pray for people in the pews during the altar call who didn't make their way to the front of the church. Besides, this was all about sharing the good news of the gospel and winning souls for the kingdom. So, who cared about a team as long as I was on God's team, and what a blessing that was. God was prophetically using me, and I certainly didn't want anyone to go to hell.

I was also on the cleaning committee, nursery ministry, and a part of the street ministry. My husband recorded live concerts in the studio. We traveled with the church choir and praise team on tours.

My husband and I both were faithful members. But something still didn't sit well with my spirit. My husband and I soon left that ministry after many years of serving. We began to visit other churches and had to feel our way through the culture shock of worshiping at all-black churches again. It all felt familiar, warm, and fuzzy. But the novelty of being visitors got old quick. At times we had nowhere to go, but I felt free. During the period that we were searching for another church, I drew closer to God even more and explored who I was as a Believer of Jesus Christ. What was my purpose in life?

There were no fillers like ministries and committees of which to depend. But in the workplace, God was using me to pray with and for people all the time. If someone wanted prayer, they came to me. I was known to be the lady that could get a prayer through from vice presidents to executives. I was bold about prayer and recognized that a relationship with God was taking flight differently. I was starting to feel confident and secure in who I was in Him. Acts 17:28 reminds us, "For in Him we live, and move, and have our being; as certain also of your own poets have said, For we are also his offspring." Wow! I just get excited to know that we are His offspring and I guess those prayer services with my knees hurting were molding me to be the prayer warrior I am today. Praise God!

Have you ever felt lonely even when you thought people in your family, church family, or on your job were a part of your tribe or circle? However, sometimes this would become a place to experience hurt and rejection. At the former ministry where my husband and I served, these were the people that I thought were pure and holy. There was one time my husband and I went back to the old church to visit for Sunday morning service, and I had never experienced so much rejection like we felt that Sunday. Even people who genuinely knew us and loved us seemed reluctant to speak to us. I'll always remember that time, but I have definitely forgiven. It was that pivotal moment that I was intentional about seeking a genuine and authentic relationship with Christ. And it has been a long journey.

The moral of my story is that I have learned that there can be a fine line between religion and a relationship with God. Or is it a fine line? Could they be further apart than we think? With years of seeking God through prayer, worship, and studying the word for myself, I know that my religious experience was a strong foundation when I was young. It is an experience I will forever be grateful for, but there comes a time in your spiritual walk that you have to dive deeper and know Him for yourself. What I've learned most about my relationship with Christ, is that He is so much bigger than the box religion we put Him in. And a relationship with God allows Him to be everything the word says He is. Everything!

The makeup and hairstyles, hats and long dresses, what not to wear and what to wear, and what colors are appropriate, in my opinion, had nothing to do with the heart and my longing to have a relationship with the Father. But let me be clear, I never want to take anything away from church culture, which is beautiful. Religion was just so conflicting with my spirit and who I know God to be in my life. But while there were many beautiful messages preached and bible teachings, you always heard about what you could and could not do. I just couldn't correlate the two. The message of love I felt in my heart when it came to salvation and winning souls has always meant everything to me. I believe that all things should be done in moderation as men and women of God. And there are countless verses in the bible that support our call to be moderate. "Let your moderation be known unto all men" (Philippians 4:5).

Remember, when I told you that I could not participate in school activities. This was no fault of my parents; they too walked in what was taught to them. My parents understood differently, but they remained faithful and obedient to the ministry. I must admit that not being able to be a cheerleader or play sports or attend school activities left a tiny scar. But by the grace of God, that tiny scar healed through my divine relationship with the Father. I know my parents only wanted to protect me from sin. My parents and I would travel across the country every summer, which always made up for what I couldn't do. We had great family times together. I vividly recall an incident with one of my sons while going on a youth trip. The rule was that you couldn't wear shorts. Because he was a kid, I wasn't thinking about the rules. It was the middle of summer; the youth were going to an amusement park with a water park. My son had recently had a spirit-filled encounter with God during a youth summer camp, and he was excited about the trip. However, he too, had experienced a youth leader calling him out as if he had done something wrong. This broke my heart. We worked through another tiny scar, but I started to see the pattern. Now that my sons are older, we've had long talks about how religion can be so damaging to a person's soul. I am thankful for the relationship they now have with God. They, too, have had to learn who God is in their life.

I hope you will see that religion can choke out everything Christ came to the earth for us to receive. Religion can be an organized system of beliefs, rules, and ceremonies, and good works that we live by and use to worship. Sometimes that's needed, but when it gets in the way of a genuine and authentic relationship with Him, it can be harmful. It's called "church hurt" for many. It is that tiny scar that becomes a long-lasting wound. How many souls have walked away from the church building because of religion? I now understand that having a relationship with God, you begin to see things through his eyes. You are putting your faith in Him, no matter the outcome. It is imperative that you invite Him in every part of your life. "I am the vine, ye are the branches: He that abideth in me and I in him, the same bringeth much fruit: for without me ye can do nothing" (John 15:5). This kind of relationship sounds like a relationship I want to be a part of, and I pray that you, too, will have the same desire.

Date: _____

Lesson One: Discovery
Discovery and Reflection Journal
The Tiny Scar that Healed

What resonated about the Author's story with you and why?

At the beginning of the Author's journey, which began in the church, in a loving home, what shifted for her? Can you relate to such a shift?

Date: _____

Lesson Two: Reflection
Discovery and Reflection Journal
The Tiny Scar that Healed

In the story, when did there seem to be a shift for her? What was the change? When you look at your own story, was there ever a time that you had a similar experience? If so, how did it make you feel?

In Minister Hope's story, she shares that at one point, she did not know the difference between religion versus relationship; she just knew church. Write your experiences. Has it changed at all over time? If so, explain the change you have had or want to have.

Date: _____

Lesson Three: The Journey
Discovery and Reflection Journal
The Tiny Scar that Healed

If you found that the above exercise was helpful, what has it taught
you about yourself, religion, and about your relationship with God?

Date: _____

Lesson Four: The Shift
Discovery and Reflection Journal
The Tiny Scar that Healed

Were you able to uncover any scars hanging around, perhaps not
healed completely? If so, list them here. If you have already won the
battle, write your victory shift statement.

Date: _____

Lesson Five: The Relationship
Discovery and Reflection Journal
The Tiny Scar that Healed

You made it another step on a "Divine Shift". The Author's central theme was centered around prayer. How has your prayer life changed? Have you found room to build your relationship with God more through prayer?

ALWAYS THERE FOR ME

Elder Berthanna Oxendine

Father God, I give you Glory and Praise for each day in my life. From the very beginning, you were there and brought me forth. My mother was at Memorial Hospital in Johnson City, Tennessee where it all started. At my birth, my father had a decision to make, between my mother's life or mine; however, he told them to save both for he could not choose, no matter the cost. So, therefore, out of my five brothers and one sister, I cost five hundred dollars more. A specialist was needed to help with delivering me into the world. My mother said I would start to come and then stop, which was affecting her heart. But once the specialist got involved, he got me moving, and finally I came, looking just like my daddy, they said.

After I was born, my mother said I would just pass out for no reason, something concerning my heart. I remember my mother telling the story how one day she and my grandmother were listening to Oral Roberts on the radio. This particular day he was praying for the sick. She said I was around one year old at the time. I got off the couch and laid my hand on the radio, and the problem I had with my heart and passing out went away.

Later in life, when I should have gotten childhood diseases, I did not get them like my brothers and cousins. Mother said I was too mischievous, or God's healing hand was still on me. Now I have learned God's hand is on us before we even get here. "Before I formed you in the womb, I knew you; Before you were born, I sanctified you; I ordained you a prophet to the nations" (Jeremiah 1:5).

As a child, I always seemed to be the oddball. I remember taking a field trip with the school. They furnished the drinks, and all the children chose orange or grape, but I decided on a Sprite. One of the teachers asked the other why are you drinking orange. I overheard her say you know the odd one; she did not want orange, but Sprite. The same teacher that called me the odd "one," was the same teacher that taught me Psalm 121 and encouraged me to never forget it. I would sometimes think that's why she taught me that scripture because she realized I needed specialized help again, verses 1 and 2, especially "I will lift up mine eyes unto the hills from whence cometh my help. My help cometh from the Lord, which made heaven and earth" (Psalm 121:1-2). I thought, help to get here, help to stay here.

I remember not being allowed to go certain places and do what other children did. My mother seemed to be so hard on me, but not my brothers. It seemed they would get away with murder, and I just did not understand. I would think to myself, *God, my mother says you see all we do, you know all and love us all.* So, if the Lord knew everything, why did God let her be my mother. I just did not understand, and I thought maybe at birth, that's why I did not want to come. Notably, when I felt unloved, rejected, and unwanted, or when my mother told my father at my birth that he should have chosen her, then, they could have had more children. So, I thought she never wanted me from the beginning.

You see, when I went through feeling rejected, I would go to a picture hanging on the wall in the corner of the living room. The picture showed Jesus as the Shepherd guiding His sheep and carrying one lamb in His arms. In my mind, I would imagine that lamb was me. I felt so safe and loved in that place. I found myself looking at that picture a lot. In reality, it was my punishment corner. In that corner, Jesus became my best friend. In my moments of being in the corner and talking to Him, I felt he was really with me. I know my mother loved me, but I believed my father loved me from the beginning because he did not want to lose me.

Over time, I came to understand things better. I had thought of things in my way, being very selfish, just thinking about my feelings, never considered my mother's feelings. There were things I knew nothing about, I would learn later in life. God does see all. Absolutely nothing is hidden from Him, nothing in all creation from God's sight. "Everything is uncovered and laid bare before the eyes of Him to whom we must give account" (Hebrew 4:13b).

I was taught the Lord's prayer and the twenty-third Psalms at an early age and baptized at the age of seven. The pastor of the church, Pastor Summilin, would have me sing before she preached every Sunday. I did not want to sing because no one else was ever called up to do it. I sang with the rest of the children when it was time. I just did not understand why she chose me.

"Jesus wants you to do it because He knows you love Him," she would say. She was right. I did love Him, and I knew He loved me, but I did not want to be in front of people. I heard her tell my mother, "You know God has His hand on her life and will use her one day." I thought, *What is she talking about using me? Who would want me or want to use me?*

In our home, my mother played the bible on records, and we had to listen every day. Sometimes, we had to say bible verses before we ate; but we always said grace before we ate. My mother was a stay-at-home mom who lived a religious life, and I saw God provide for our home, I believe, because of her prayers. Early every morning, I would hear her praying and crying out to God. I am talking about miracle-working prayers where we would sit down for dinner with nothing cooked and say grace. I would begin to think mommy had lost it. There was nothing to say grace over. Then we heard a knock at the door; someone brought food. That was the best chicken and rice we had ever tasted. I realized she was walking a walk that I did not yet understand. The Milkman would leave milk, and the bread man left bread, even when the bill was overdue.

One day the landlord and his wife wanted some lamb, and my mother cooked it for them, and the months we were behind on rent, wiped away, forgiven. I know my mother was praying over that lamb while cooking it, as she did when cooking anyway. I began to realize that God loved my mother and listened to her. He even gave her favor with man. She was a woman living by faith, not by sight.

Once when my dad got laid off from work, my mother got a day job working for this Doctor's family. One particular morning, my mother came home early that scorching summer day and made all of us come inside and would not let us go back outside. My dad told my two oldest brothers to go to the store and get him a pack of cigarettes. Mother said God showed her something was going to happen to one of her children that day. She said, "I want them close to me." My dad did not want to hear all that stuff. If we were going to the store, my mom decided I would go too. My two-year-old brother wanted to go, and my mother had a fit because my dad said to let him go. Then, she gave us his thick snowsuit with the cap to put on him, and we did.

The clerk at the store knew us; he asked why my brother had all of that on as hot as it was? I said my mother told us to put it on him. He looked at us so strangely. "Tell your mother to call me," he said. On the way back from the store, one brother held my little brother's right hand, my other brother held his left hand, and I stood behind him with my hands on his shoulders to keep him from breaking loose again as he had done before. We were almost home and were holding tight. All safe, then some way, suddenly, my little brother got loose and ran up the street, then across the street, and got hit by a car. The car knocked him up in the air, and the Dayton Power light heavy-duty company truck ran over him. The driver radioed for help. One of my brothers ran to our house. My other brother and I pulled my little brother out of the street to the curb.

When my mother saw my brother run into the house, she fainted. One ambulance took my mom, and another took my little brother, and my dad got us. The hospital was about seven to eight miles away, and at the time, my mother was nearly six months pregnant. I remembered just saying, *"Lord, have mercy,"* repeatedly in my insides. Lord, give her one of her miracles and let us go home. I wanted to get to my safe place.

I remember someone said, "This is one of our caseworkers, and your children will be going with her." My mother started screaming, "You cannot have my children." She began grabbing for us, even me. What a joy I felt inside during a bad situation. The priest was coming down the hall to my brother's room to do the last rites. My mother began just screaming, "Lord, please have mercy." The doctor and nurse were trying to talk to my mom to calm her down. We were crying and holding onto mom.

Everything was happening so fast, so much confusion. Then the priest came out of the room and asked, "Where is the father of this child?" I do not know where my father came from, but he and the priest went into another room. When they came out, the priest and doctor went back into my brother's room. My mother was still saying Lord, please have mercy. Then the doctor came out of the room, and another miracle happened. My brother's vitals had begun to change, and they were taking him to surgery. It took my brother about three years to walk again without help. The doctor said the cushion in his snowsuit padded him, but he was still crushed severely. Once again, God saved.

They did not take us from our parents, my father started going to church with us, stopped drinking, started working again, and my little brother was still with us. When my brother was able to come home, nuns took him to a convent in Cincinnati, Ohio, to continue praying over him. They took me too, because he would cry by himself. So, my mother sent me with him. I remember sitting on a bench in an area like a courtyard while waiting for my brother. The Nuns would walk around, just praying with a small book in their hands. It was so serene and peaceful there. I liked going to the convent and having the ability to watch them pray.

The first time I visited the convent, the nuns gave me a doll with a black uniform like theirs on it. The last time I was there, they gave me another doll with an all-white uniform. They hugged me so tight before I left, and told me they loved me and to remember that God loves me too. I thought maybe this is where I am supposed to be with all this love and peace, the same feeling I had in front of my picture. I held on to those dolls so tight, but my relationship with my mother still did not change.

Every time she prayed, I would see God move for her. Just like when I wanted a sack dress like the other girls in school, my mom told me we could not afford to buy you one. "Lord, if you want her to have one bring her one." I, of course, was not thinking of all the financial obligations they had. My dad said he would try to find someone to make me one, if he could. I knew he would try because whatever he told me, he always kept his word. Well, guess what happened? The Goodwill truck came with not one, but three spanking, brand new sack dresses just for me! I thought I had hit the jackpot! Oh, my goodness, another miracle just for me, God must love me.

At two years old, we moved to Dayton, Ohio. I was a Buckeye girl until I graduated High School in 1972, and I said I am out of here. Because no matter how hard I tried, my mother and I seemed to not get along. Our communication was through whippings, standing in the corner, or being grounded. There were no parties, no prom, and no graduation activities. The time had come; my mind, for sure, was made up, and I was leaving.

Tennessee, I'm coming home, back where it all started. However, my plan and God's plan were not the same. I thought I was going to get loose and free, to do whatever I wanted, but little did I know His hand was still on me. I wanted to do whatever I thought I had missed. I tried to go to the club, but the owner saw me coming in and said, "This is not your place, this is not a place for you, and I cannot let you in!"

I was shocked; Why just me again? I said, "That is not right." All he said was, "I am sorry, sweetheart; I will not do it!" I can remember wanting a certain kind of drug, but those trying to get it to me, got picked up by the police. I said, just forget it. I give up! I soon realized that when my mother and others said no, it was for my protection. All was for protection from things designed to hurt and keep me from God's plan. Proverb 3:5-6 says, "Trust in the Lord with all your heart and lean not to your understanding but in all your ways to acknowledge Him, and He shall direct your paths."

I have now learned the enemy will attack; however, he cannot abort God's plan for you. God is right there all the time. In the very beginning, He was the specialist that brought me into the world. It was God that was in a stern mother that said, "No," but showed me the power of prayer. He was also the father that understood me. He was in a Pastor that chose me to sing; He was in my teacher that taught me the Lord is your help. He was in a caseworker that caused my mother to grab for me. The Lord was in the nuns that hugged me so tight and gave me the dolls that I would cherish. I could see

Him in the Club owner that turned me away. He even had a Gideon bible open in a hotel room, that would speak the words, *Thou shall not commit adultery.* And many, many more ways He has shown me He was always there.

I rededicated my life to my Friend and asked why He allowed me to go through some things and not others. He said, *I know what I can trust you to go through and come through.* Psalm 119:71 reminded me that it was good that I was afflicted; that I might learn thy statutes. I realized I was in love with what I saw, the acts of God, and the many miracles, time after time. I loved God for what He did, not who He is! A lot of times, we know He is with us by the good we see. But now, I recognize He is and has always been there for me. He made known his ways unto Moses, his acts unto the children of Israel (Psalms 103:7).

Date: _____

Lesson One: Discovery
Discovery and Reflection Journal
Always There for Me

In this chapter, let's review what resonated with you about the Author's story and why.

At the beginning of the journey, did the Author realize that God was always there?

Date: _____

Lesson Two: Reflection
Discovery and Reflection Journal
Always There for Me

Where in the story did there seem to be a shift for her? When you look at your own story, was there ever a time that you were not sure God was with you?

For Elder Oxendine, it was the tough love of her mother that she was able to forgive as she learned. Look inward and ask, is there forgiveness that I also need to release into the atmosphere, so that I can live in the plan God has for me?

Date: _____

Lesson Three: The Journey
Discovery and Reflection Journal
Always There for Me

If you found that the above exercise was helpful, what has it taught you about yourself and about God in your life?

Date: _____

Lesson Four: The Shift
Discovery and Reflection Journal
Always There for Me

You took a bold step in all the lessons above, if you were brave enough to do the work. It is time now to begin the shift. As you went through the "why" questions in the above lessons and from what you have learned about yourself, how can you shift your mindset to Trust God even when you don't understand Him?

Date: _____

Lesson Five: The Relationship
Discovery and Reflection Journal
Always There for Me

You made it another step on a "Divine Shift." How has your vision of your life changed? Have you found room to build your relationship with God and yourself more?

PAIN DESIGNED FOR PURPOSE

Juanita Corry Jackson

Jeremiah 29:11 " For I know the thoughts that I think toward you, saith the LORD, thoughts of peace, and not of evil, to give you an expected end.".

Pain always comes with a price! It is a prophetic warning and is always intended to produce within us a travel schedule to a place called purpose. Wow! Check out the five P-words: pain, price, prophetic, produce, and purpose. Pain is often misunderstood; it is like the stepchild, not the bounce child. Pain attaches itself to an emotion that is designed to get our attention. Pain, although it is a warning, can be loud and boisterous. I have not ever seen anyone with a diagnosis of pain. Disclaimer: I am not a physician, nor do I hold a degree in any form of clinical medicine. This is a message I gained in obtaining my (PPD) Pain, Purpose, Driven Degree. It was earned through the school of hard knocks my grandmamma would say.

I learned that although the pain was what I was experiencing, it was attached to the emotion of feeling, which could land in my mind, heart, ears, or body. However, the pain was trying to get a message to me. Perhaps there had been warning signs before, and I ignored them. Okay, I'm sure there had been warning signs that I totally ignored. Why would I or anyone, for that matter, ignore a prophetic warning? The reason, it is the natural, or the most comfortable thing to do. No one likes what Iyanla Vanzant would call "the down in the gutter truth." No one wants the down in the gutter change. The kind of change that has the power to turn your world upside down. This is when things around you are not recognizable anymore.

I recall this scripture to mind, Jeremiah 4:19 KJV, "My bowels, my bowels! I am pained at my very heart; my heart maketh a noise in me; I cannot hold my peace, because thou hast heard, O my soul, the sound of the trumpet, the alarm of war." This scripture represents an aching of the heart of the Prophet Jeremiah. It described a pain that was inexpressible, as grief was all around him. His heart seemed to have a disorder of confusion that could not be explained. At the same time, Jeremiah wanted to express this feeling of heartache and disarray. Have you ever felt that confusion, pain, and emptiness, yet the words would not come to give it a true meaning of what you felt? I can say I had many days like this. When something bothered me so badly, it was unnerving, if you will. However, there was also a set of religious rules that made it seem impossible to speak.

I was seventeen years old when I conceived my first child, and I was single. On top of this earth-shattering fact, my mom and stepfather were Pastors. I remember, there seemed to be one set of rules for the Pastor, and their family and then another set of rules for everyone else. When I told my mom, not much was said, accept a child is a blessing. My two siblings and I were born out of wedlock, only no one ever addressed it as such. It was the thing everybody knew but was not allowed to talk about it. When the word got to the church about my pregnancy, one lady told my parents that I would have to sit down and would not be able to work in the church. My parents agreed, and instantly, there was that down in the gutter change. No more singing in the choir, no more ushering in the church, no more anything, except going to church, and sitting near the back. I am not sure what that did for me at all. It certainly did not help redeem me in any way.

So here I was, about to become a teenage mom. No love, no compassion from all the people who supposedly knew more than I, not even one class to help show me the right way. Let me just say that from the bible perspective, sin is wrong! Here is a news flash though, all sin is counted the same. No matter your age, race, nationality, or gender, it is all the same. Even at seventeen, I was fully aware that premarital sex was wrong, so I am not condoning it. What I am saying, is that when I formed a relationship with God, I realized that God loved me unconditionally. He had already decided that he had a plan for my life.

I learned that God forgives sinners. "In Him we have redemption through His blood, the forgiveness of sins, in accordance with the riches of God's grace" (Ephesians 1:7). Did you hear that, God's

Grace, not man's Grace? The same lady who decided I would sit down, all of her children had been born out of wedlock. Yep, that's right, but it was before she became a devout, religious leader. However, not long after my first child was born, she became pregnant again—still, no husband in sight. Did she sit at the back of the church? Absolutely not. She did sit on the back row of the choir though. Then there was the married deacon who tried to hit on every woman in a skirt. What is the moral of the story? These were just flawed people who caused pain in my life and maybe even their own. I have come to know that this is the kind of pain we typically label as "church hurt." In reality, these two people were not the church, and my relationship with God was never supposed to be predicated on either of them.

As an adult with a total of three children later. My pain was a warning that ended up costing me a high price. The Price: I did not fully understand that I was repeating a generational curse. Oh my God, my mom had three children and no husband when we were born. My grandparents raised us. I promised myself that when I had children, I would be there, no matter the cost. They would know that I loved them, and I would be fully present in their life. I kept good on my promise. While I conquered one half the battle, the other half, I fell forward on that step. I use falling forward instead of mistakes because I believe that it is a teachable moment; I can learn and keep moving forward. Anyway, I digress. I kept becoming attracted to the same kind of man who was not the right man, willing, ready, or able to step up to be the Father or king our family needed. Part two of the curse was continued. I have taught this principle over and over to my children, and my testimony is they got! Thank you, Jesus!

Maybe to the lady with the religiosity way of thinking, I was just a reminder of her own pain. At any rate, it's not important now, because that's not how my story ends. I kept working in the church, and I kept growing. I was determined not to give up on God, even when I had to give up on people, because God never failed me. In my early years, one scripture I would hold on to was about the lady in the bible caught in adultery. I am paraphrasing here, but referencing St. John 8, when the Pharisees, the religious leaders, brought this woman to Jesus citing the law. This woman was not named in the scripture; they told Jesus she was caught in the act of adultery, and the law called for her to be stoned.

Thank God I'm not Jesus, because my question would have been, Where is the man? Adultery takes two people, even in the bible days. Okay, but Jesus being graceful as He is, does not take the time to be petty, calling out the fact that the man was not brought to Him. He just writes and ignores them. The Pharisees would not let it go, though, they just kept insisting. He simply tells them in His Jesus kind of way; you are right according to the rules. Go head; he that is without sin cast the first stone, and just goes back to writing. Lord, Have Mercy! As old people would say, I bet you couldn't hear a pin drop. When Jesus looks again, only the woman was left. Jesus said to her, where are your accusers? Of course, none were there. Why, because the bible says that we have all sinned and come short. Baby, every one of us has sinned and come short. So, Jesus says, then neither do I condemn you. Go and sin no more. Do you understand how powerful that is even now? This lady had to pay the price of shame, dragged out in front of all these religious leaders. According to the law, she was guilty, but God! His words have creative power.

God already knew she was not perfect, but the people who brought her before Jesus were not perfect either. In this scripture, it re-enforces that He came to die for me, to redeem me from sin. I too paid a price.

In the beginning, I told you how I had to sit at the back of the church, and everything that I did in the church at the time, was stripped from me. Even later in life though, I bounced back, I got married, and things seemed to be on the right path. There was still more pain that I would have to endure—marital infidelity, a child born as a result of that infidelity, then divorce. Then starting a new life, with virtually no income, but again I say, but God!

The Prophetic comes to give knowledge, warnings, wisdom, or pronounce a future. "For I know the thoughts that I think toward you, saith the LORD, thoughts of peace, and not of evil, to give you and an expected end" (Jeremiah 29:11). I have read this scripture many times and never saw it this way before. Yet it is all here, knowledge, warnings, wisdom, and the pronouncement of a future.

- For I Know-says that God has knowledge of something that I do not. The fact that there is a plan that has been designed for my life means I will not be aware of all the details.
- The Lord has thoughts of peace and not evil. Check the warning, and the evil thoughts are not coming from God, it is from another source.
- Wisdom—no matter what it looks like right now, this is not how the story ends. God is going to give you something that you don't have yet.
- Pronouncement of the future-It is an expected end, my end has not arrived yet, I can rest assured that this future will

come because Jesus himself expects to arrive. Coupled with the office of a Prophet, according to Jeremiah 1:10, is to uproot, tear down, destroy, and overthrow, to build and plant. Look at the pain, the price, the prophetic, the produce, and purpose.

The Prophet does not stop at the pain; the Prophet goes to the root of what is causing the pain and uproots it. The fact that it is destroyed and overthrown says that even though it caused me pain at the time, if left unattended, it would have eventually killed me. It was not in God's plan for me, so he causes the enemy to be destroyed. All this could leave a hole, a hallowed place; then, this must be filled so that the emptiness does not also destroy me. Then the Prophet must begin to build you and prepare for planting. The planting stage is still fragile and must be nourished, watered, and watched with care. Thereby, the Prophet is called a watchman. All of this, I now understand as part of my relationship, is that God is always producing something to help us reach that expected end.

Produce: This you will find, I believe, an alone season. When the seeds go in the ground, they are put into a dark place. They are mistaken by most people, except for the person who does the planting, as nothing of importance. To the natural eye in the beginning stages of becoming, people count you out, less than even. After all, you look like nothing but dirt. You get walked on, and no recognition of your future self. See, it takes vision and faith to plant something in the dirt and expect it to come back to you more significantly than you left it, but God does!

Then when harvest time comes, everyone wants to circle back and get in on the harvest. Remember, your gifts could not be seen in the dark. Sometimes in the dark, we don't understand our giftings either. We sometimes just can't see or understand when we are engulfed in the middle of the storm. My gift, your gift, once it is stirred and developed in you, is supposed to produce something in you. That is why the bible tells us that our gifts will make room for us! It has been through something to propel me to the next dimension.

Purpose: I am walking out today what I know right now to be my purpose, but this too, is not where the story ends. Today I Pastor a church; I oversee several ministries and partners of our International ministry. I am a bestselling Author, a certified consultant with Les Brown Maximum Achievement Team, and the ATS Bureau of Dominant Speakers. I have a real estate business, and I am a Trainer, and Coach. My children are grown and in their own homes. I have one granddaughter that the enemy tried to take from us too soon, but God! In all this, my purpose is to lead and teach other Faithpreneurs how to have a clear vision by disrupting the norm and releasing the Spirit of God's freedom to flow in their God-given gifts.

I learned that the rules of religion are just a set of rules made up of flawed people. I have learned that His Grace is sufficient for me. His Grace comes to give me what would be impossible for me to earn, and His Mercy protects me from what I deserve. This kind of a relationship with a Sovereign all Powerful God takes the time to talk with me and tell me that I am His own. For my sins, He died. I am now part of His royal family, and He calls me friend. This makes every storm worth it, and I just touched the surface here. It makes the dark place, when I could not see, I could not understand, all worth it! There were times when I felt alone, even when I started to see the gift move in my life, no one else could see it, but God did. He always had a plan for me, even when I didn't know. Because of Him, I am enough, because He is still more than enough. God has no respecter of persons; what He has done and is doing for me, He will do it for you! It's in His Plan. My Pain was always predestined to get me to my purpose!

Date: _____

Lesson One: Discovery
Discovery and Reflection Journal
Pain Designed for Purpose

In this chapter, what resonated about the Author's story with you and why?

At the beginning of the journey while the Author had a relationship with God, there was still pain experienced. Why was that?

Date: _____

Lesson Two: Reflection
Discovery and Reflection Journal
Pain Designed for Purpose

*Have you experienced what we have labeled as church hurt? If so,
how did you handle that pain?*

If you have experienced church hurt, or pain from whatever the source, what did the pain teach you?

Date: _____

Lesson Three: The Journey
Discovery and Reflection Journal
Pain Designed for Purpose

Forgiveness is the first step to complete healing. Did you forgive the offender?
If so, how? If not, write them a letter explaining how you feel. Then release them through forgiveness in the letter. Remember, forgiveness is more for you than the other person.

Date: _____

Lesson Four: The Shift
Discovery and Reflection Journal
Pain Designed for Purpose

You took a bold step in all the lessons above, if you were brave enough to do it. It is now time to begin the shift. Pain is a warning sign. What did you learn about the five P's, and how can you use it to shift your mindset in the future?

Date: _____

Lesson Five: The Relationship
Discovery and Reflection Journal
Pain Designed for Purpose

You made it another step on a "Divine Shift." Has your vision of your life's purpose changed? Every storm we come through is meant to help someone else. Have you found room to build your relationship with God, yourself, and others through your purpose?

Date: _____

Lesson Six: My Story
Discovery and Reflection Journal
Divine Shift

Five Stories and thirty-one life application Lessons. From "A Pathway to Forgiveness," we learned to "Choose Love," that "The Tiny Scars That Healed," that God was "Always There For Me," and my "Pain Designed For Purpose." Now it's your turn, what is the title of your chapter, your own personal Divine Shift? Write as much or as little as you want.

The Discovery is what happened, and when you realized that God was using what happened to shape you.

Reflection: is when I can look back on the facts that were meant for my bad, but God Turned it for my good.

The Journey: my process of healing, which must include forgiveness.

The Shift, God, has or is transitioning me from the pain to purpose.

Relationships, because of the life lesson, I can now see the growth in my own life.

If you would like to share your story in our "Divine Shift" Author Group, you can do that by joining:

https://bit.ly/DivineShiftGroup

ABOUT THE AUTHORS

Deloris J Washington

Deloris was born in West Virginia in the era of World War ll and Jim Crow Law. She moved to New York shortly after graduation, to marry the love of her life. After completing Nursing School, she began a career in many facets that nursing affords. During her career, she had the opportunity to testify before the Congressional Health Care Committee to include Senator Edward Kennedy and local Congressmen on behalf of Families USA. This allowed her to help bring awareness of the needs of families who provide long-term in-home health care for family members. Deloris is now widowed after 45 years of marriage. She is the Mother of three children, five Grandchildren and many young men and women who fondly call her Mom.

Over the years, she became a Certified Sunday School Teacher, Home Bible Study Teacher, Volunteer Christian Chaplain, and presently serves as a Certified Cancer Care Specialist. She currently serves as coordinator of the Hospitality staff at Abundant Life Church.

Bishop Dr. Valerie J Rogers

Bishop Valerie J. Rogers is the Pastor of New Beginning Deliverance Ministry where she has served for the past 14 years. She currently serves as Director of Education with the I Believe God Ministries International, Inc. Bishop Rogers attended the Upper Room Bible College and Seminary and has received her Doctorate Degree in Biblical Studies. Bishop Rogers is the mother of  2 children; Jeanine Boston, Jeremel Boston, and she raised her nephew Bobby Washington. She has 10 grandchildren and 4 great-grandchildren.

Bishop Rogers is a Proverbs 31 woman, called by God to serve the people of God. She walks in the office of a Prophet, Teacher and Pastor.

Minister Angela A Hope

Angela A. Hope is a proud Washingtonian now living in Charlotte NC, where she enjoys her entrepreneurship lifestyle. Angela is a financial wellness advisor, helping people across the country, restoring, rebuilding, and  protecting their credit, among other diversified services to leverage financial well-being. Angela has supported C-suite executives for nearly thirty years in law, media, entertainment, and financial services with Viacom and the NBA. Angela is now owner of A Hope and Company LLC, a virtual administrative, concierge, and talent acquisition service

She genuinely loves her family and loves sharing life with her best friend, who happens to be her beloved Husband, Malkin Hope. Together they enjoy their beautifully blended family of two sons and three daughters and six grandchildren.

Elder Berthanna Oxendine

Berthanna S. Oxendine, is the Senior Pastor of Open Door Tabernacle Training Center, in Johnson City, TN. She also serves as the Administrator for I Believe God Ministries International, Inc. Berthanna is the Co-Owner of Rose of Sharon Wedding & Essentials and serves as Wedding Director. Pastor Oxendine has founded a prayer line to help restore love, faith, and deliverance. She is currently a Liaison working with  the Board of Ellis Johnson Community Center to reopen formerly known as the girls and boys club.

She is a graduate of Paul Lawrence Dunbar, a wife, mother, grandmother, and great grandmother. Along with these accomplishments, she now holds the title of Co-Author.

VISIONARY AUTHOR

Overseer Juanita Corry Jackson

Juanita Corry Jackson is the CEO of Creative Global Management Solutions, Inc. She is a Bestselling Author, a certified Speaker, Trainer, and Coach. Juanita also serves as Overseer of I Believe God Ministries International, Inc and the Pastor of I Believe God Ministries Charlotte.

Juanita is an entrepreneurial, dedicated, skilled business professional, and a natural solutions-oriented leader. Juanita has developed her leadership, training, and development skills through many diverse organizations and Industries. Juanita brings a wealth of knowledge from Health Care Management, Real Estate, Ministry, along with Training and Development.

She has helped leaders and teams reach their full potential, while also assisting companies to improve revenue margins and workplace productivity.

Juanita is the mother of three children: Demond, Shareka and Kendra, and one grand-daughter Taniyah. More importantly, she is a woman of faith; she is a Transformational Vision Specialist.

Made in the USA
Monee, IL
25 October 2020